globe-trotters CLUB

Saudi Arabia

Laurie Halse Anderson

Carolrhoda Books, Inc. / Minneapolis

Photo Acknowledgments

Photos, maps, and artwork are used courtesy of: John Erste, pp. 1, 2–3, 14–15, 21, 25, 30–31, 38–39; Middle East Pictures, pp. 4, 6, 7, 8, 9 (both), 11, 12, 13, 16, 17 (top), 20, 22 (bottom), 23 (top) 26, 27, 28, 29, 32, 36, 37 (both), 38, 39, 40, 41, 42, 43; Laura Westlund, pp. 5, 27; © TRIP/TRIP, pp. 10, 17 (bottom), 18, 19, 22 (top), 33, 34, 35; © Tor Eigeland, pp. 14, 15; © Camerapix/ Middle East Pictures, p. 21; © Wolfgang Kaehler, p. 23 (bottom); © TRIP/OP, p. 24.

Cover photo of detail of painted door © Erik Bjurström/Middle East Pictures.

Copyright © 2001 by Carolrhoda Books, Inc.

All rights reserved. International copyright secured. No part of this book may be reproduced, stored in a retrieval system, or transmitted in any form or by any means—electronic, mechanical, photocopying, recording, or otherwise—without the prior written permission of Carolrhoda Books, Inc., except for the inclusion of brief quotations in an acknowledged review.

Carolrhoda Books, Inc.
A division of Lerner Publishing Group
241 First Avenue North
Minneapolis, Minnesota 55401 U.S.A.

Website address: www.lernerbooks.com

Words in **bold type** are explained in a glossary that begins on page 44.

Library of Congress Cataloging-in-Publication Data

Anderson, Laurie Halse.
    Saudi Arabia / by Laurie Halse Anderson.
       p. cm. — (Globe-trotters club)
    Includes index.
    Summary: Examines the geography, history, economy, society, and culture of Saudi Arabia.
    ISBN 1-57505-121-4 (lib. bdg. : alk. paper)
    1. Saudi Arabia—Juvenile literature. [1. Saudi Arabia.] I. Title.
II. Series: Globe-trotters club (Series)
DS204.A67 2001
953.8—dc21   99-16276

Manufactured in the United States of America
1 2 3 4 5 6 – JR – 06 05 04 03 02 01

Contents

Ahlan wa Sahlan fi as-Sa'udiya	4
Across the Country	6
Deserts and Oil	8
Family Life	10
Who Are the Saudis?	12
The Bedouin	14
Urban Saudis	16
Islam in Saudi Arabia	18
Muslim Life	20
What to Wear?	22
Kid Life	24
A Trip to the Souk	26
Speaking and Writing	28
Poems and Stories	30
Schooldays	32
Let's Eat	34
Saudi Art	36
Music and Dance	38
Time to Celebrate	40
Fun and Games	42
Glossary	44
Pronunciation Guide	46
Further Reading	47
Index	48

Ahlan wa Sahlan fi as-Sa'udiya

*That means "Welcome to Saudi Arabia!" in Arabic.

Saudi Arabia covers most of the **Arabian Peninsula.** The country is in the **Middle East,** the part of Asia that meets Africa and Europe. The world's twelfth largest country, Saudi Arabia is about the same size as the United States east of the Mississippi.

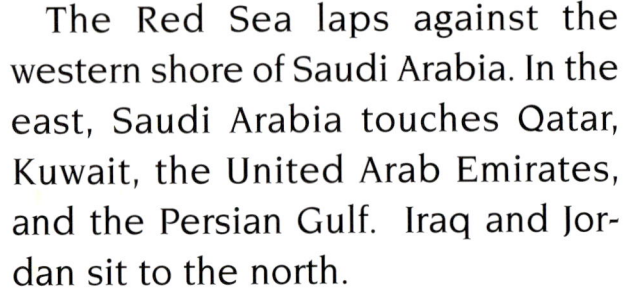

The Red Sea laps against the western shore of Saudi Arabia. In the east, Saudi Arabia touches Qatar, Kuwait, the United Arab Emirates, and the Persian Gulf. Iraq and Jordan sit to the north.

Southward lie Oman and the Republic of Yemen. The southern border of Saudi Arabia is marked by a dotted line. That's because there isn't a way to clearly mark the **desert** to show where one country ends and another begins. Deserts blanket most of Saudi Arabia. The country also boasts mountains, green valleys, and farmland.

Rocks and sand stretch across a Saudi Arabian landscape.

mountains
highlands
lowlands
deserts
undefined borders
capital city
N
IRAQ
JORDAN
KUWAIT
PERSIAN GULF
QATAR
UNITED ARAB EMIRATES
AL-NAFUD
ARABIAN PENINSULA
AL-HASA
HEJAZ
SAUDI ARABIA
Medinah
NEJD
Riyadh
RED SEA
Jidda
Mecca
ASIR MOUNTAINS
ASIR
TIHAMA PLAIN
RUB AL-KHALI
OMAN
YEMEN
INDIAN OCEAN
Miles
0 100 200 300
0 200 400
Kilometers

Across the Country

A hiker pauses at the edge of a Hejaz canyon.

The people of Saudi Arabia—the Saudis—divide their land into several regions. Hejaz runs along the Red Sea's coast. Beaches and cliffs rise to rocky hills and mountains. Farmers raise coffee, grains, vegetables, and fruit on the Tihama Plain, south of Hejaz. Inland, visitors find the beautiful Asir Mountains. Saudis have terraced the slopes so that farmers can use all of the good soil. In the lowlands, farmers grow bananas, papayas, and lemons. Almond, pear, and fig trees and grapes fill the fields higher in the mountains. Shrubs dot the craggy peaks.

A huge, rocky plateau region called the Nejd stretches eastward. Thick-haired sheep roam the Nejd. The sheep eat tough shrubs that can survive desert heat. When it rains, water fills **wadis,** streambeds that are dry for most of the year.

Lush, green **oases** dot the Nejd, where most Saudis live. Oases support date palms, gardens, and entire cities, such as Riyadh. In ancient times, traders traveled from oasis to oasis to cross the desert. North of the Nejd, a desert called Al-Nafud meets Jordan and Iraq. The reddish sands of Al-Nafud form huge **dunes.**

Fast Facts about Saudi Arabia

Name: Al-Mamlakah al-'Arabiya al-Sa'udiyah (the Kingdom of Saudi Arabia)
Area: 865,000 square miles
Main landforms: Al-Nafud, Rub' al-Khali
Highest point: 10,279 miles in the Asir Region
Lowest point: sea level
Animals: Camels, sheep, goats
Capital City: Riyadh
Other Major Cities: Jidda, Mecca
Official Language: Arabic
Money Unit: riyal

Green farms cover the terraced hills of this village in the Asir Mountains.

Desert winds have blown rippled patterns into the sand.

Deserts and Oil

A huge desert called Rub' al-Khali (the Empty Quarter) covers southeastern Saudi Arabia. Enormous sand dunes ridge Rub' al-Khali, where wind races through the dunes to make an eerie sound called "the singing sands." Rub' al-Khali is the biggest sandy desert in the world—it's about as big as the state of Texas. It's also the driest, hottest place on earth. During the day in the summer, temperatures of 120 degrees can make thermometers explode!

Salt flats and gravel plains border the Persian Gulf. About one-fourth of the world's oil lies beneath this dry steppe, called Al-Hasa. The landscape is filled with machines that pump the oil to the surface.

Rain hasn't fallen in the Empty Quarter for more than 10 years. Saudi Arabia averages only about four inches each year! Even so, the Asir can get 20 inches of rain a year.

Pipes and valves mark the location of an oil well.

Watch out for sandstorms! A sandstorm can blow sand at 30 miles per hour for days. The sand can blast the paint off buildings and knock over trees.

Family Life

Saudi families are very close. Kids usually live with their mom and dad. Aunts, uncles, cousins, and grandparents often live nearby. The whole family probably gets together at least once a week.

According to tradition, men and women have very different roles in Saudi Arabia. Men go to work, take care of the shopping, and run errands. Women raise children, help care for older family members, cook, and run the household. In modern times, some women attend college and find jobs outside the home. They tend to choose jobs that keep them around other women.

A proud Saudi father brings his children to play at the park.

Saudis are used to a separation of men and women in everyday life. Saudi women are more comfortable in the company of other women. Saudi men can relax more around other men.

All in the Family

Here are the Arabic names for family members. Practice using these terms on your family. See if they can understand you!

grandfather	*jeddee*	(ZHED-ee)
grandmother	*jeddatee*	(ZHED-ah-tee)
father	*eb*	(EHB)
mother	*omun*	(OH-moon)
uncle	*omi*	(AAHM-ee)
aunt	*omti*	(AAHM-tee)
brother	*okh*	(OAK)
sister	*okht*	(OH-kit)
son	*wuld*	(WILD)
daughter	*bent*	(BINT)

11

Saudis in traditional outfits and North American–style clothes mingle on a market street in Jidda.

Who Are the Saudis?

About 20 million people make their homes in Saudi Arabia. Most Saudis are **Arabs.** Arab families have lived on the Arabian Peninsula for thousands of years. Saudi families are grouped into **clans,** which belong to tribes.

In the past, each tribe defended an area of the country. **Sheikhs** and councils ruled the tribes. In modern times, 80 tribes live in Saudi Arabia. Some tribes are small, and others are big. Most Saudis are very proud of their clan and tribe.

Naming Names

Saudi names tell about a person's family. A boy's name is followed by "ibn," which means "son of," and the name of the boy's father. Girls' names are followed by "bint," and the name of her father. Saudi Arabia's first king is usually known as Abd al-Aziz ibn Sa'ud. But his full name was Abd al-'Aziz ibn 'Abd ar-Rahman ibn Faysal ibn Turki 'Abd Allah ibn Muhammad al Sa'ud. Can you figure out his great-grandfather's name?

Answer: Turki 'Abd Allah

Guest workers make up nearly 4 million of the people of Saudi Arabia. Guest workers are people from other countries who work in Saudi Arabia. And a small number of Saudis are foreign Muslims (followers of the religion Islam) who decided to settle in Saudi Arabia.

A man from the Tihama Plain wears the traditional headdress of his clan.

The **Bedouin**

Before oil was discovered in the 1930s, more than half of all Saudi Arabians were Bedouin, or **nomads.** These days about 10 percent of Saudis are nomads who herd goats and sheep and move from place to place with the seasons.

Saudi culture comes from Bedouin traditions, such as generosity to guests. Generosity is a desert custom because no one can live alone in the harsh desert. A guest in a Bedouin tent is treated like family. The hosts offer water, food, clothing, and shelter—everything needed to survive.

The Bedouin used to weave tents from black goat hair, although in modern times people choose tents

Diners prepare to dig into a Bedouin meal.

A Bedouin herder grazes his flock in the Nejd.

made from high-tech fabric. Tents provide shelter from the hot sun. Because the walls don't go all the way to the ground, cool breezes can blow into the tent. Modern-day Saudi nomads stay near schools and hospitals so that kids can be educated and sick folks can be treated.

White buildings crowd this Riyadh neighborhood.

Urban Saudis

About 70 percent of Saudi Arabians live in cities such as Riyadh and Jidda. Modern buildings made of cement, glass, and steel line wide streets. Many buildings are white, which helps keep the structure cool by reflecting (not absorbing) sunlight. Saudi Arabia's cities boast schools, hospitals, roads, shopping malls, airports, grocery stores, parks, and soccer stadiums. Many buildings have shady courtyards, where people can relax. Cities also have beautiful gardens with fountains and pools of water, which add moisture to the dry air.

Urban Saudis usually live in houses or apartments. The homes usually have two living rooms, one for men and one for women. In

Saudi Arabia, men and women only mix together if they are related. In the living rooms, folks sit on luxurious woven carpets and pillows on the floor. Some families pick couches and sofas. Urban Saudis usually work close to home so that they can join their families for the midday meal. Kids get out of school in time to eat lunch at home, too.

A man strolls by a cool fountain in an office building's courtyard.

Beautiful carpets cover the floor and comfortable cushions line the walls in this Saudi home.

17

Islam means "submission" in Arabic. Muslims submit (give in) to the will of God.

Islam in Saudi Arabia

Islam is the religion of Saudi Arabia. Islam is the basis for Saudi daily life, law, government, education, and much more. All Saudi Arabians and many guest workers are Muslims.

Muslims believe that the prophet Muhammad received God's messages. These became the Koran, the holy book of Islam. It includes some stories found in the holy books of Judaism and Christianity.

A Saudi woman pauses to say a short prayer.

Many Saudis prize antique, hand-written Korans decorated with rich fabrics and colored drawings.

Muslims use a calendar called the *hijri* (emigration) calendar. It dates from the year 622, when the prophet Muhammad led his followers to the city of Medinah. According to the hijri calendar, a month lasts for a full cycle of the moon. Saudi Arabia has an observatory where the official sighting of the crescent moon is made. The new month cannot begin until the crescent moon is seen.

A Holy Time

Ramadan is the holiest month to Muslims. Muslims can't eat or drink from sunup to sundown during Ramadan, when they stay up late for a big meal. Schools and shops are closed for most of the day.

Muslim Life

Muslims believe in the Five Pillars of Islam. The pillars are five religious duties that Muslims must perform: *shahada* (the Muslim declaration of faith), *salaat* (prayer fives times a day), *zakat* (giving to charity), *sawm* (fasting during daylight hours in the holy month of Ramadan), and *hajj* (a religious visit to Mecca at least once in their lives).

Muslims pray at dawn, noon, mid-afternoon, sunset, and nightfall—five times in all. All business stops at prayer time. Prayers only take 10 minutes, but they are very important. Muslims wash themselves before praying. All Muslims face Mecca—the holiest city of Islam—when they pray. Guess where Mecca is. Saudis are proud that Mecca is in Saudi Arabia!

This mosque, like most others, has a tall tower called a minaret. Traditionally a singer climbs the minaret to call people to prayer five times a day. In modern times, many minarets have large loudspeakers that broadcast the message.

The **mosque** is the Muslim place of worship. The Muslim holy day is Friday, when many families go to the mosque for noon prayers and to hear the **imam** preach on Fridays.

Mecca's Great Mosque attracts large numbers of hajj visitors each year. The black structure in the mosque's inner courtyard is called the Kaaba. Muslims walk around the Kaaba seven times to complete their hajj.

sawm

zakat

hajj

salaat

shahada

What to **Wear?**

Most Saudis wear traditional clothing. Men wear a *thobe*, a thick white shirt that goes all the way to the ground. In cool weather, men wear a *bisht* (a woolen cloak) over their thobe. On their heads they wear a large piece of cloth called a *gutra*, which a black cord called an *agal* holds in place. Bedouin men originally used the agal to tie camels. The cord kept a man's gutra in place while he traveled, and it kept his camel in place while the man slept!

Saudi women wear veils that cover their faces *(above)*. **Many Saudi men cover their heads with a gutra** *(right)*, **a square of cotton cloth folded diagonally.**

Women always wear clothes that cover their arms and legs. Many pick beautiful, brightly colored outfits. But in public, women wear a black, robelike *abbayah* over their clothes. It even covers their faces! When women are with female friends, they can take off their abbayahs.

Women wear their abbayahs to go shopping for new carpets.

White is a popular color for Saudi clothing. In the hot sun, a white thobe is cooler than dark-colored clothing would be.

Kid **Life**

The **extended family's** love surrounds a Saudi child. Families help kids decide what to study at school, what kind of job to have, and who to marry. Kids respect their older relatives and follow their advice.

Usually boys hang out with boys and girls hang out with girls. Free time is for playing with cousins and friends. Saudi kids play soccer and run around in cool courtyards. Indoors, children play video games and board games.

After school, Saudi boys play a quick game of soccer.

Some boys join the Boy Scouts, who help the hajj pilgrims. They earn merit badges for desert camping skills and for training falcons to hunt. Girls aren't scouts, but they learn crafts from relatives, friends, and schoolteachers.

Islam is important to Saudi kids. They look forward to being old enough to fast during Ramadan. They usually can fast when they're about seven years old. Kids celebrate the first time that they read the whole Koran. At bedtime kids listen to stories about the founding of Islam and the first followers of the prophet Muhammad.

Popular Pets

The cat is the number-one pet in Saudi Arabia. Other popular pets include rabbits and birds. Some kids keep pigeon coops on the flat roofs of their homes.

You won't find a dog in anyone's home—they aren't considered clean enough to come indoors. Dogs are farm animals and live outside, where they can guard sheep.

Buyers and sellers bargain over fresh-caught seafood.

A Trip to
the Souk

A **souk,** or marketplace, is one of the most exciting places in a Saudi Arabian city. If you visit, you'll hear chickens clucking and merchants laughing. The air smells of spices, coffee, and incense. Fires crackle under grilling lamb. Gold jewelry flashes in the sun. Fancy daggers, embossed leather, and handmade carpets are all for sale. Coppersmiths pound copper into beautiful coffeepots.

Haggling is an old tradition in Saudi souks. No one pays the advertised price for an incense burner or pearl earrings. The shopper and the merchant bargain back and forth until they agree on a price.

In small towns or villages, the souk may be the only place to shop! City-dwellers can go to an air-conditioned shopping mall instead. You'd probably feel at home in a Saudi mall. Like malls everywhere, these have shiny escalators, video arcades, and "sale" signs in the windows. Shops sell clothes and goods that you might find in North America. They also sell the type of merchandise found in a souk.

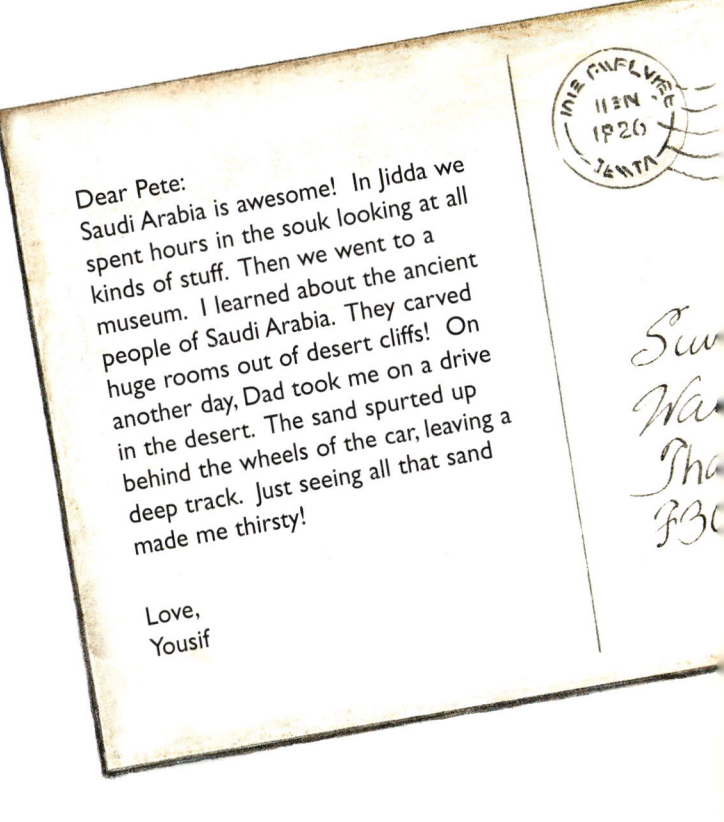

Dear Pete:
Saudi Arabia is awesome! In Jidda we spent hours in the souk looking at all kinds of stuff. Then we went to a museum. I learned about the ancient people of Saudi Arabia. They carved huge rooms out of desert cliffs! On another day, Dad took me on a drive in the desert. The sand spurted up behind the wheels of the car, leaving a deep track. Just seeing all that sand made me thirsty!

Love,
Yousif

A gold merchant helps customers at his store in a shopping mall.

Speaking and **Writing**

In the back of his car, a businessman jots some notes.

The language of Saudi Arabia is Arabic. Writers in Arabic don't use the same alphabet as writers of English. There are 29 letters in the Arabic alphabet. Unlike English, letters don't indicate vowel sounds in Arabic. Instead, vowels are shown with little marks above and below the consonants.

People write Arabic from right to left. Readers turn book pages from left to right. That's the opposite way that English-language books read. To Saudi Arabian readers, English-language books look backwards!

But English speakers and Arabic speakers use the same system of numbers. Long ago, Arabs borrowed the idea of using numerals from people in India. Arab traders passed the idea to Europeans.

Some English words are from Arabic.

Atlas, banana, and camel came from the Arabic words atlas, banan, and jamal.

The Saudi Arabian Flag

The flag of Saudi Arabia has a sword and a sentence in Arabic. The sword shows that Saudis will fight to spread and to defend Islam. The Arabic words translate to "There is no God but Allah, and Muhammad is his prophet." This is one of the Five Pillars of Islam. The flag's background is green, the color of Islam.

Poems and Stories

Saudis love poetry! They chant it, listen to it, write it, and read it. Poetry readings are broadcast on TV and on the radio. Saudis enjoy ancient poems about brave adventurers in the desert. Bedouin history is retold in poems about daring camel raids and heroes who uphold tribal honor. And Saudis write poems in modern times.

Some tales with Saudi roots are famous across the world. The stories may have larger-than-life heroes, such as Sinbad the Sailor. He is said to have sailed on the Red Sea and visited Jidda. Many Saudi Arabian stories tell of genies. The word "genie" comes from the Arabic *jinn*, a spirit that blows across the desert. Some Saudi **folktales** tell how parts of nature came to be a certain way.

Who lied?

A Bedouin tribe once looked for new grazing land for sheep. The Bedouin sent the crow, the partridge, and the dove to search. The crow returned and said that he found only desert and no grass. The other two birds returned and said exactly the opposite—that they had discovered enough lush grass to feed all of the sheep. The tribe followed the partridge and the dove and found what they said was true. Because the crow had lied, they painted him black. The Bedouin rewarded the partridge by lining her eyes with kohl (a dark eye makeup) and the dove by painting her feet pink.

School Days

Boys work on art projects as their teacher gives advice.

In Saudi Arabia, classes start at six in the morning. School begins early so that students can avoid the hottest part of the day. Even though the schools are air-conditioned, the heat outdoors can still make rooms feel stuffy.

Boys and girls go to separate schools. They study math, Arabic, history, science, and Islam. Girls also learn how to cook and to sew, while boys take gym. School ends at one in the afternoon, when kids head home for lunch. The school year lasts from September to June.

Teachers use the Koran in many classes. For handwriting class, kids copy verses from the Koran. Social studies classes study it to learn Saudi law. Schools hold competitions to see who can recite the most verses from the Koran. And when a child has read all of the Koran for the first time, the whole class celebrates with a party. In some towns, the kid gets a parade through the school.

Girls listen to taped lessons in a language class.

A selection of Saudi dishes tempts the appetite—*(from bottom left, counterclockwise)* a relish tray, tabbouleh, pita bread, and baba ganouche.

Let's **Eat!**

This morning many Saudi children ate a bowl of cereal and drank a glass of juice for breakfast. On weekends families usually have more time. Then they enjoy traditional breakfasts of tabbouleh (lettuce and tomato salad), hummus (mashed chickpeas), and goat cheese.

Lunch is the biggest meal of the day. Saudis gather at home for lunch. They might eat lettuce, cucumbers, tomatoes, lamb stew, and rice. A family living by the Persian Gulf might choose freshly caught fish. After lunch many people rest for a few hours. It's too hot to do much else! Children who don't want

You'll find McDonald's in Saudi Arabia. The menu has foods that Saudis like to eat.

to take a nap might read or do their homework.

For a light dinner, Saudis can choose pita bread with hummus or baba ganouche (eggplant dip). Others munch deep-fried crescent-shaped pies filled with meat, cheese, or spinach.

Coffee Break

Serving tiny cups of coffee, often spiced with cardamom, is a Saudi custom. The oldest or most important person is served first. People nibble dates between sips of the unsweetened coffee. Saudis consider it polite to drink two cupfuls, but not three! To refuse the third serving, a Saudi waggles the cup back and forth to say "no." And after everyone finishes drinking the coffee, it is time to go home.

Saudi Art

It's hard to lug fancy pieces of art around when you keep packing up your tent and moving on. So nomadic Saudis created beautiful everyday objects, such as carpets and embossed leather saddles for camels and horses. They hammered out graceful coffeepots and incense burners. Saudis treasure these objects in modern times as well.

Many Saudis admire beautiful jewelry. As wedding presents, Bedouin women receive gold jewelry to show their wealth. Many Saudis wear five bracelets or rings—

Saudi Arabia is famous for its colorful carpets and woven cloth items.

five is considered a lucky number. Children like to wear bell-trimmed bracelets and anklets.

Many cities feature sculptures that show parts of Islamic and desert traditions. A big sculpture of a Koran stand that holds the holy book arches over the road leading to Mecca. Sculptures of coffeepots and incense burners more than six feet tall are grouped in front of modern buildings or made into fountains. The art shows that although Saudi Arabia is very modern, the country's people value symbols of their traditional culture.

A man displays an incense burner for sale in his shop (above). A sculpture shows a huge chest of jewelry at the center of a public fountain (right).

Music and Dance

The national dance of Saudi Arabia is the sword dance, called the *ardha*. Men stand shoulder to shoulder in rows and face the same direction. In the center of the group, a poet sings while drummers beat a rhythm. The men step and sway, waving their swords in the air. Big or small groups can do the ardha.

Traditional coffeepots, rugs, and cushions surround a Bedouin man. He plays an old-fashioned string instrument called an *oud*.

Most regions of the country have different versions of the ardha. Some dances are competitive. Men line up in two facing rows. One at a time, each man steps forward to perform different dance steps. The man opposite must copy or even improve the steps.

Traditionally music hasn't played a major role in Saudi life. But many Saudis tune into a TV program that shows performances of the music of every tribe and village in the country! Musicians sing and play traditional folk instruments, such as the lute and the *tar* (a goatskin drum).

The sword dance is an opportunity for Saudi men to show off their fancy footwork.

39

Fireworks light up the sky at the end of Ramadan.

Time to **Celebrate!**

A three-day festival marks the end of Ramadan. Families attend prayers in the mosque. Then they go home to exchange gifts and enjoy a feast. Many people wear new clothes. Saudis give gifts to the poor. In the Asir, women repaint their bright pink, blue, or yellow houses.

Saudis celebrate their culture with the Janadriyah Heritage Festival, which lasts for two weeks each

Camel races are fun for riders and spectators alike.

March. People display crafts such as leather work and weaving. Musicians play and people crowd poetry competitions to hear poets recite famous verses. Each poet has memorized pages of ancient poetry. They try to outdo each other by reciting it in a lyrical, rhythmic way that will enchant the listeners. Dancers perform the ardha.

The Great Camel Race begins the Janadriyah Heritage Festival. More than two thousand camels and their riders race in front of the king. Some riders are professionals, but any male—even young boys—can enter. Camel jockeys need a good sense of balance to stay in the swaying saddle. They try not to anger their camels because the animals spit!

Fun and **Games**

There are no movie

Falconers spend lots of time training and practicing with their hunting birds.

Soccer is the most popular sport in Saudi Arabia. Can you imagine practicing when it is 115 degrees? It wouldn't be much fun, so soccer players go to gyms. Saudis enjoy watching international soccer, too. Basketball is the newest sport to watch. It's more popular in Saudi Arabia every year.

Centuries ago Bedouin warriors rode horses when battling rival tribes. Those horses became the modern Thoroughbreds, the fastest breed of horses in the world. In

theaters in Saudi Arabia! Instead, people watch videos and television at home.

modern-day Saudi Arabia, many people love to cheer at horse races. Another favorite traditional sport is falconry. Owners release the trained falcons (a fierce bird of prey), which catch and kill other birds. Then the falcon flies back to its owner's wrist. Falconers follow strict rules about training and caring for falcons.

For fun on the weekend—Thursday and Friday—Saudi families might camp in the desert. Saudis pack a tent, plenty of water, and drive to a favorite spot. They usually nap through the hottest part of the day and stay up through the cool night. For a trip to a cooler spot, they might visit Asir.

A picnic in the desert makes a fun Friday evening for a Saudi family.

Glossary

Arab: A person who speaks Arabic, belonging to the ethnic group from the Arabian Peninsula.

Arabian Peninsula: The Arabian Peninsula lies in southwestern Asia, bordered on the west by the Red Sea, on the east by the Persian Gulf, the Arabian Sea, and the Gulf of Aden (parts of the Indian Ocean). To the north sit the countries of Jordan and Iraq.

clan: A group of families who have a common ancestor.

desert: A dry, sandy region that receives low amounts of rainfall.

dune: A hill of sand piled up by the wind.

extended family: Mothers, fathers, brothers, sisters, grandparents, aunts, uncles, and cousins who often live together in one household.

fasting: Going without eating or drinking.

folktales: Traditional stories told for generations.

imam: Muslim religious leader and prayer leader of a mosque.

Middle East: The countries in North Africa and Southwest Asia from Libya in the west to Afghanistan in the east.

mosque: Muslim place of worship.

nomad: A person who moves from place to place, following seasonal sources of water and food.

oasis: A place that has water and vegetation in the middle of the desert.

plain: A broad, flat area of land that has few trees or other outstanding natural features.

plateau: A region of level land that is above most of the surrounding territory.

Ramadan: The ninth month of Islamic year, this the holiest time of the year for Muslims. It is a time for fasting from dawn to sunset.

sheikh: An Arab chief or tribal leader.

wadi: A streambed that is dry for most of the year. When it rains, wadis flood with water. Many run down mountainsides.

Masub

Masub is a sweet, mushy dish that children of the Asir love to eat on chilly days.
You will need:

2 honey-wheat English muffins
1 ripe, peeled banana
1/3 cup water

2 tablespoons honey
1/2 tablespoon butter
1 teaspoon lemon juice

Tear the untoasted English muffins into nickel-sized pieces. Mash the banana with a fork until there are no chunks. Mix the water, honey, and lemon juice in a microwave-safe bowl and microwave it for 45 seconds. Be careful when you take it out—it will be hot! Stir it until the honey dissolves. Add the mashed banana and the bits of muffin. Stir it again until the mixture is blended. It might look a little yucky, but that's okay. Stir in the butter, and microwave it for another 30 seconds. You're done! Serve the masub before it cools down. Try it with a little milk poured on top.

Pronunciation Guide

agal	UH-gahl
Ahlan wa Sahlan fi al-Sa'udiyah	AH-*lehn* WAH SAH-*lehn* FEE *ah-sah-oo-DEE-ah*
Al-Hasa	ahl-HAH-suh
Asir	a-SIHR
Bedouin	BEH-doo-ihn
bisht	BISHT
gutra	GOO-truh
hajj	HAHJ
Hejaz	heh-JAZ
Ibn	IHB-ihn
Id al-Fitr	EYE-eed AL FEHT-reh
Janadriyah	jah-nahd-REE-yah
Jidda	JIHD-dah
Koran	koh-RAHN
masub	mah-SOOB
Mecca	MEHK-kah
Nejd	NAJD
oud	OOD
Ramadan	RAH-mah-dahn
Riyadh	REE-yad
salaat	suh-LAHT
sawm	SAHWM
shahada	sah-HAH-dah
souk	SOOK
tabbouleh	tuh-BOO-leh
tar	TAHR
thobe	THOHB
Tihama	tee-HAH-muh
zakat	zuh-KAHT

Further Reading

Al-Hoad, Abdul Latif. *We Live in Saudi Arabia.* New York: The Bookwright Press, 1987.

Dutton, Roderic. *An Arab Family.* Minneapolis: Lerner Publications Company, 1980.

Foster, Leila Merrell. *Saudi Arabia: Enchantment of the World.* Chicago: Childrens Press, 1993.

Haskins, Jim. *Count Your Way Through the Arab World.* Minneapolis: Carolrhoda Books, 1987.

Moritz, Patricia M. *Dropping in On . . . Saudi Arabia.* Vero Beach, FL: Rourke Corporation, Inc., 1998.

Saudi Arabia in Pictures. Minneapolis: Lerner Publications Company, 1999.

Williams, Marcia. *Sinbad the Sailor.* Cambridge, MA: Candlewick Press, 1994.

Metric Conversion Chart

WHEN YOU KNOW:	MULTIPLY BY:	TO FIND:
teaspoon	5.0	milliliters
Tablespoon	15.0	milliliters
cup	0.24	liters
inches	2.54	centimeters
feet	0.3048	meters
miles	1.609	kilometers
square miles	2.59	square kilometers
degrees Fahrenheit	5/9 (after subtracting 32)	degrees Celsius

Index

Al-Hasa, 8
animals, 6, 14–15, 25, 31, 41, 42–43
Arabian Peninsula, 4, 12
art, 36–37
Asir Mountains, 6, 7, 8, 40, 43

Bedouin, 14–15, 22, 30, 31, 36, 38, 42

carpets, 17, 23, 36
celebrations, 19, 25, 33, 40–41
cities, 6, 16–17
clothing, 12, 13, 22–23, 40

dances, 38–39, 41
deserts, 4, 6, 8–9, 14–15, 30, 43

families, 10–11, 17, 24
farmers, 6–7
flag, 29
folktales, 30–31
food, 6, 14, 17, 26, 33, 34–35, 45

guest workers, 13

haggling, 26
Hejaz, 6
history of Saudi Arabia, 12–13, 42
houses, 12, 16, 17, 40

Islam, 13, 18, 20, 25, 29, 33

Janadriyah Heritage festival, 40–41
jewelry, 27, 36, 37
Jidda, 12, 16, 30
jobs, 10, 13, 24

Koran, 18, 19, 25, 33, 36

languages, 13, 28, 33

map of Saudi Arabia, 5
Mecca, 20–21, 37
mountains, 6–7
Muhammad, 18–19, 25, 29
music, 38–39, 41
Muslims, 13, 18–19, 20–21

Nejd, 6, 15
nomads, 14–15, 31, 36

oasis, 6
oil, 8–9

people, 10–11, 12–13
Persian Gulf, 4, 8, 34
pets, 25
playtime, 10, 24–25, 42–43
poems, 30–31, 41

Ramadan, 19, 20, 25, 40
Red Sea, 4, 6, 30
religion, 13, 18–19, 20–21, 40–41
Riyadh, 6, 16
Rub' al-Khali, 8

sand dunes, 6, 8
schools, 10, 15, 17, 24, 32–33
shopping, 10, 12, 23, 26–27
souk, 26–27
sports, 24, 42–43
stories, 25, 30–31

tribes, 12, 31, 42

weather, 6, 8–9, 32, 34

48